THE HUMANITIES AND
THE COMMON MAN

THE HUMANITIES AND THE COMMON MAN

The Democratic Role of The State Universities

By

NORMAN FOERSTER

CHAPEL HILL
THE UNIVERSITY OF NORTH CAROLINA PRESS
1946

Copyright, 1946, by
The University of North Carolina Press
Printed in the United States of America
Van Rees Press · New York · PJ

PREFACE

THE HIGHER OUR conception of human nature, the higher will be our conception of education. The lower our conception of human nature, the lower our conception of education.

The high rôle of the state university, as an instrument of American democracy, is to bring the humanities to the common man. Its most distinctive duty is to enable the common man to enter into his cultural heritage, to develop his own humanity by means of it, to learn to face life with a sense of relative values, to prepare for his part in dealing wisely with the desperate problems of the next half century. Under existing conditions no other agency can do this, not the press, not the radio, not the motion picture. To do it for a significant portion of the people is the great function of undergraduate education at the people's university.

What we commonly have today, however, is a low view of human nature and of education. While professing ideal purposes, those who control our state universities have generally followed a working program based on the assumption that man is essentially a materialist desiring bread and circuses. During four pleasant college years student activities are supposed to provide something like circuses, while student passivities—submission to training for a vocation—promise bread after graduation. The average student, it is implied, has little or nothing of importance to gain from such things as armchair philosophy, polite literature, and the dead past. "Culture," in this view, is not for the common man; he does not want it and cannot be made to want it. He is right in being practical, in going after direct utility. He should be trained for a job—everything else is incidental.

But this, I am going to suggest, is to conceive of him as a

slave. The utilitarian specialists who control most of our state universities are not content that the common man should be a worker: he should be nothing else, he should be kept a mere worker. They will not recognize and develop his humanity. They refuse to provide a way to make him free. They want to draw the young man or woman into a vocation as early as possible, "adjust" him more and more firmly in an occupational groove, make of him a slave to society ("one for All"). When in the nineteenth century the lower classes seemed about to arrive, the old order said, "We must educate our masters." Today a newer old order says, "We must educate our slaves," shape them into more useful slaves. Or even worse, into things, "parts" for an intricate machine. This cynical view is justified to the student himself by an appeal, equally cynical, to his self-interest. He is invited to regard the university as a vocational school for getting him on in the world ("all for One"). To be sure, the utilitarian specialists do not always say these things so frankly. In university catalogues they actually speak of "the well-rounded development of the individual," and everywhere they proclaim their views, disarmingly, in the name of democracy.

In belying man's freedom they are not justified by the facts of science—of biology and psychology. Whenever the facts seem to reduce man to a low plane, they have been colored by an admixture of philosophy, and philosophy, of course, is not science. We are as free as ever to believe in the nobility of man, and must believe in it if we are to keep civilization a going concern. There is no occasion for any new or old myth. We need not, in the manner of the demagogue, flatter the common man as an angel complete—if he were, there would be small occasion for religion and education. We need only believe that there is a noble element in every man because he is a man, however overlaid and obscured by laziness, by all other vices, by the effect of a bad environment. Men at their worst sink even beneath animality, and yet remain men, moral creatures, potentially superior to lower forms of life. Only moral beings can be immoral.

The very word *humanities* (the plural of *humanity*) should remind us that they concern all humankind, are not exclusive, not for any class, not for an artificial aristocracy of birth or wealth, not for a natural aristocracy of intelligence, but for all men and women. They concern all of us, concern us more deeply than anything else, concern our very humanity. Humanity—this is the very common thing which the common man possesses as truly as the uncommon man. Because of it every man (as Jefferson conceived, as Henry Wallace conceives) has uncommon potentialities. Humanity is the most important thing about the common man, and about his education.

As an example of a democratic recognition of the common man I may mention a course in great literature given for more than a decade at a state university. At the University of Iowa, beginning in 1933, a two-year course was required of all freshmen and sophomores. Conceived as a unit, it dealt with a few of the great books of the Hellenic and Hebraic-Christian foundation of our civilization: Homer, the Greek tragedies, Plato, the Bible, together with works of Chaucer, Shakespeare, and later English and American authors to suggest the continuity of the tradition. It was not a historical survey, nor a study of literary art; it was a study of human values. Through constant analysis and discussion relating past and present, through constant "themes" stimulating a definite and personal response, the course explored the possibilities of the good life and aided the student in his effort to work out for himself a conception of life and a scale of values. When use was made of "sectioning according to ability," students in the "low" sections demanded the right to follow the regular readings instead of a denatured program. Fortunately tolerated by a university faculty aiming at quite other ends, the course was deplored only by a few specialists who paid it the compliment of saying that it unsuited the student to merely utilitarian purposes.

All men desire the good life, however, inadequate or perverted their notions of goodness. Because of their inherent capacity for nobility, they can be attracted to what is excellent. A main function of education is to direct their desire for excellence toward objects that are really excellent. There is excellence in our own modern world, despite its mass production of suffering, and this excellence should be communicated. There was excellence of other kinds in the religious and humanistic ages of the past, and this too should be communicated. The best things thought and made and done in the past were not just a mark of aristocracy; they were given to the world, and are a heritage not for the few but for the many, not a means of education for a decorative class or group, not a way of escape from our own age, but the most available practical means of educating the common man in self-realization, largeness of understanding, and ability to meet contemporary needs. The concept of "best" may take us anywhere and anywhen, because it is not limited by time or space. In the view of culture, ours is one world.

Since men differ widely, it is not to be supposed that all will derive the same results from their contact with the humanities. "To each acording to his talent." The humanities can be grasped on many levels, and are amply rewarding, as experience shows, even on a very low level of understanding. To say that what is great is for the few is to insult the common man, to deny the element of greatness in his nature. He has a stake in spiritual as well as material wealth. The century of the common man calls for a better distribution of material wealth; it needs, no less, a better distribution of spiritual wealth.

Acknowledgments are due a number of persons who kindly read the manuscript: Seymour M. Pitcher, James B. Stroud, Austin Warren, René Wellek, of the State University of Iowa; W. R. Boyd, of the Iowa State Board of Education; Nicholson B. Adams, L. C. MacKinney, and Harry K. Russell, of the University of North Carolina. I am also indebted to The University of North Carolina Press for permission to reprint as a separate book what first appeared as the concluding chapter of a volume entitled *A State University Surveys the Humanities*, which was issued as part of the Sesquicentennial Celebration of the oldest state university, the University of North Carolina.

Chapel Hill   N.F.
June, 1945

P.S. Had the Harvard report, *General Education in a Free Society*, been published before my own little study went to press, I should doubtless have been much indebted to it. At the least I would have included it prominently among the books named on page 56.

CONTENTS

Preface	v
I. Human Values	3
II. The Spirit of the Humanities	5
III. The Naturalistic University	10
IV. Educationists	18
V. New Forces	21
VI. The Heritage of Free Men	29
VII. Liberal Education	32
VIII. The Great Curriculum	37
IX. The Great Faculty	45
X. The Great Administration	51

THE HUMANITIES AND
THE COMMON MAN

1. Human Values

AMERICA ENTERED THE war to defend democracy against fascism, civilization against barbarism, the humanities against the inhumanities. It was not to be a meaningless war of things, of machines and material resources, but a war of men against men, of mind against mind, of will against will. It was to be a war of human values.

The values believed in by the enemy were all too clear; the values we believed in, all too vague. The Four Freedoms were essentially negative—freedom from religious intolerance, controlled opinion, fear, and want. If freedom could be won and extended, what positive aims were to direct the use of it? No clear affirmations came from our political leaders, or even from those peculiarly responsible, leaders in the fields bearing the proud name of "humanities": historians, men of letters and art, philosophers, churchmen. In the war of values they promptly went on the defensive. They called upon us to "preserve" our way of life, the liberal arts, the humanities, often in a tone that implied only "business as usual." They appeared not to realize the seriousness of the failure of the modern world of science and democracy to achieve new values or to deepen the vitality of old values. They spoke as if unaware that the modern world, interested in multiplying the instruments of living and in distributing them more equitably, has been living upon the spiritual capital of the past, and that this spiritual capital has steadily depreciated. While professing to despise the wisdom of the ages, indeed the past and all its works, we have continued to use our heritage of values, or rather to use it up. The human values that we have taken for granted are nowise different from those of the past, the values founded for Occidental civilization by Greece and Judea, but they have grown more and more attenuated, surviving in ever feebler forms. The coming of the war did not reverse this process. To the crude naturalistic aims of the enemy we were unable to oppose any clear aims of an affirmative and commanding sort. We derived strength adequate for the conduct of the war from our negative aims: our hatred of the painfully clear aims of the enemy, our determination to destroy the menace of those aims. The forces of darkness and indecency must first be halted—then we would set about the advancement of light and decency. And we were clear, at least, that the winning of the war must somehow be followed by the winning of the peace.

Before us lies the long, hard task of winning the peace and keeping it won. This we cannot do by force alone. We shall need courage to use force if occasion demands, a courage lacking after 1918, and we shall need wisdom in the establishment of high purposes, a wisdom lacking after 1918. The burden laid upon our intelligence, our idealism, and our moral character is stupendous. I do not see how any man can reasonably predict our success. Nor do I see how any man of good will can refrain from the effort to do his part to bring about success. Everywhere we shall need men of intelligence and character, both leaders and followers, in industry, in politics, in journalism, in law and medicine, in scientific and humanistic research, in the church, in education. Nowhere do responsibility and opportunity lie more plainly than in the field of education, as modern democracy has always understood even if it has left full demonstration to the totalitarian nations. As never before, we must place our hopes and our striving in education, the education of children, of youth, of adults. Within the field of education, nowhere do responsibility and opportunity lie more plainly than in the public or state universities.

In the pages that follow I shall be concerned with higher education in general and with the state universities in particular. Begun in the South, they have spread throughout the nation, taking on their most definite patterns perhaps in the Middle West. Universities of the people, they have prided themselves upon their service to democracy. In truth they have done much for democracy. They are now called upon to do far more. How much will they do, in the crucial years before us, for the advancement of human values? I shall not venture a prediction. It will be more profitable to consider rather what the advancement of human values entails, what we may understand by a humanistic spirit guiding the life of the state university, and what the conditions are that make for and against that spirit.

2. THE SPIRIT OF THE HUMANITIES

A state university is or should be dominated by a general intent, a permeating and unifying ideal, however precious the minority opinions that oppose that intent and test its validity. The intent should not be specific—sectarian or partisan—but general: it might be naturalistic, religious, or humanistic. For decades it has been in fact, I would say, naturalistic. It cannot be expected, in the present spiritual situation, and in view of the separation of church and state, to become a religious intent. But it could become humanistic.

What does this mean? To define the humanistic spirit acceptably is as impossible as to define the democratic spirit acceptably. Despite academic literalists hot for the tangibles, it seems necessary to tolerate the vagueness of such terms in order not to lose contact with truth. The two terms, as we use them today, have much in common. In contrast with fascism, the democratic and the humanistic spirit today agree in emphasizing the development of the individual. They agree in emphasizing the human as opposed to the racial or national (despite the fevers of nationalism, democracy has placed first the rights of man). They agree in demanding a society of free men. And they agree in conceiving of authority as internal, a free inner consent or dissent.

The humanistic spirit flourished, of course, long before modern democracy, flourished variously and splendidly—if not in its political aspect—under the absolute monarchy of Louis XIV, in the aristocratic Renaissance, in imperial Rome, under various polities in Greece, where it first came to fruition. Percy

Gardner has stated very simply the several stages in the development of our civilization. "Three great discoveries," he says, "lay open to the awakened spirit of man when he first began to realize and reflect upon his surroundings. The first was the discovery of God, which was mainly the work of the Prophets of Israel, though no doubt Greece added much on the intellectual side; and the religions of both Judea and Greece were carried to a higher point by Christianity. The second was the discovery of man himself, which was in all essentials the great work of Greek thinkers and writers. The third, begun in Greece, has been carried very much farther in modern times, the discovery of nature and her laws." Today the humanistic spirit cannot forget that it was Greece that not only discovered man but gave the fullest demonstration of man's capacities. It was Greece that most splendidly realized the dignity of man as man, as a being essentially different from the rest of the animal order, including, in Plato and Aristotle, an adumbration of the spiritual dignity upon which Christianity staked everything.

In the long history of the humanistic spirit, what has been the fundamental aim? From Socrates and Plato to Goethe and Emerson and persons today who are in the tradition, the aim has been self-knowledge and self-realization. The nature of the human self has been variously conceived, without doing violence to the large area of consensus within the tradition. Man is a creature, it would seem, who recognizes in his constitution a power of command, whether this is regarded as rational or ethical; a power of command over his thronging desires and passions, by means of which he shapes his desires and passions in harmonious expression. Life for him is action, external action and, even more, internal action, an inner working upon himself. The good life comes not by nature, but is an achievement based on progressive self-knowledge and habituation to what is good for his constitution. He realizes the good life not apart from men but among them, with the help of all men of good will, co-operation meaning primarily the relation of example and imitation. From the inner life flows the outer life, action taking the form of deeds, works of speculation, works of fine art, works of useful art, all institutions. The measure of all things, man himself as a complete, symmetrical being, is more important than nature, which gives him materials to work with, or the instruments of living which he fashions (such as the products of what we call technology), or any collective entity such as society, state, or folk. While perceiving that life is full of variety and change, he rests his hopes in personal and social values that are constant and enduring.

For Americans, perhaps the most suggestive expression of the humanistic spirit in relation to education is Emerson's address, "The American Scholar," happily remote from the heated debates of our own day. The marks of a changing world are in it: passages in which the humanistic spirit is given a romantic accent. But Emerson speaks mainly of and from the unchanging world of principles sound at all times. He points out how the ever-growing division of labor, while it has made man more helpful to himself, is threatening to destroy man, that is, man as a complete, symmetrical being. Man tends to become a mere tool, a thing, many things. "The tradesman scarcely ever gives an ideal worth to his work, but is ridden by the routine of his craft, and the soul is subject to dollars. The priest becomes a form; the attorney a statute-book; the mechanic a machine." (Emerson was spared the spectacle of many universities, especially state universities, more and more blithely dedicating themselves to this vocational deformation.) He goes on to describe a generous education worthy of the idea of man. In a threefold curriculum he proposes, first, the study of nature, the field of natural science—the learning of observed facts, the attempt to formulate laws of nature, the suggestion of a relationship between the laws of nature and the laws of the human mind. Secondly, he calls for the study of the human past, the field of the humanities, specifically literature, art, and institutions. Addressing the Phi Beta Kappa Society, Emerson finds it necessary to attack "the book-learned class, who value books as such," meek scholars resting in accepted dogmas as well as "the restorers of readings, the emendators, the bibliomaniacs of all degrees." But books came into the world not dead but as "quick thought," and should beget quick thought, spurring the scholar to fresh creation. "The one thing in the world, of value, is the active soul," which, however obstructed, is contained within every man. Books must be so read, so taught, that they will speak to the active soul. And thirdly, Emerson demands that the scholar recognize action, direct experience in living, as an indispensable means to vital truth. "Only so much do I know, as I have lived," he says, and, perhaps thinking of college faculties, "Instantly we know whose words are loaded with life, and whose not." Living is essential to thinking, and in the end more important. While thinking is a partial act, living is a total act. The scholar cannot afford, whether as scholar or man, to be a recluse.

Having considered the education of the scholar by nature, by books, and by action, Emerson turns to the scholar's duties, summing them up in self-trust. "In silence, in steadiness, in severe abstraction, let him hold by himself; add observation to observation, patient of neglect, patient of reproach, and bide his own time—happy enough if he can satisfy himself alone that this day he has seen something truly." He should be free (academic freedom); he should be brave, not deriving his tranquillity from his position in a protected class (security of tenure).

Nowhere does Emerson speak more plainly in the humanistic spirit than when, in recurrent passages, he asserts the unity of man. He shows his awareness, to be sure, of individual differences, "that peculiar fruit which each man was created to bear," but these differences do not contravene, for him, the essential sameness of men. The great books he finds always contemporary, or rather timeless, because "they impress us with the conviction that one nature wrote and the same reads." Again, the scholar is conceived as finding that his insight is not personal but universal: "In going down into the secrets of his own mind he has descended into the secret of all minds." Like the orator—like Emerson himself in this famous address— he begins perhaps in self-distrust and then, "the deeper he dives into his privatest, secretest presentiment, to his wonder he finds this is the most acceptable, most public, and universally true." "For a man, rightly viewed, comprehendeth the particular natures of all men." The end of a generous education would seem to be, consequently, the transformation of the young and unformed, not into adjusted members of an unsound society, nor into tools for service in ever multiplying vocations defined by the division of labor, but into mature human beings, men and women of understanding and integrity.

Emerson's conception of an education dominated by the humanistic spirit was in harmony with the great tradition from Socrates to the middle of the nineteenth century. It differed, to be sure, in omitting the authoritative sanctions generally applied by European classicism and Christianity, and in recognizing the scientific tradition of "improving natural knowledge" which had developed amazingly since the seventeenth century. Regarded by contemporaries as a forward-looking utterance, his address was heralded as America's intellectual declaration of independence, and rightly enough, since in scholarship, science, and letters the New World soon vied with the Old. But Emerson did not look forward—perhaps did not choose to look forward—to the triumph of the forces of naturalism that occurred within a few decades. Today, more than a century since his address, the humanistic view of life and of education has been almost completely displaced, for the first time in the history of the Occident, by a naturalistic view of life and of education. In theory, our break with the past is all but complete. In saying this I do not forget that in the realm of values we are, in practice, still living on our inherited capital, having acquired no other. We are daily assuming, for example, freedom of will, moral responsibility, human dignity, perhaps even ideal causes or ends more important to us than life itself. We are doing this unconsciously; we are continuing humanistic assumptions and practices because we are human. But they are in the background. In the foreground, in deliberate thought and speech, in the books, the articles, the classroom lectures, in our official philosophy that we seek to promote and put to use, our conceptions are overwhelmingly naturalistic.

3. The Naturalistic University

That this is so may be seen by drawing up a list of beliefs current in American state universities today. The beliefs stated below represent the kind of thinking which some universities have reached, others have approximated, and many others are drifting toward. Flourishing most in the Middle West and least in the South, these conscious beliefs are everywhere resisted by more or less unconscious humanistic assumptions and traditional humanistic practices. From the humanistic point of view, they constitute a set of half-truths and errors which threaten educational disaster and hence social disaster.

It is believed, as a foundation for the entire creed, that man is simply an animal, though not a simple animal. Man's place in nature has been found, and he has no other place. The difference between him and other living beings is purely quantitative. He is an organism in an environment, a bundle of drives seeking expression. Generally he is held to be "good" by nature. Evil is then the result of environment, of faulty political and social systems, probably in the last analysis economic systems. In the understanding of human nature we may safely ignore the pre-scientific "wisdom of the ages"—the humanistic wisdom of Plato and Aristotle and Confucius, the religious wisdom of Buddha and Jesus. Our view of man in the universe must come from the latest correctors of Copernicus, Newton, Darwin, Marx, Freud. Our view of human nature will somehow combine the realistic theory of Hobbes that man is characterized by "a perpetual and restless desire of power after power" with the sentimental theory of Hume that he is characterized by sympathy for his fellows, an original capacity to share in their happiness or misery, or, as John Dewey would put it, a natural desire to serve. In this humanitarian version of naturalism it is hoped, despite the evidence, that when the desire of power and the feeling of natural sympathy conflict, natural sympathy will restrain the desire of power.

It is believed, if not always asserted, that the good life of man consists mainly in the pursuit and possession of material advantages, the machinery of life, the instruments for convenience and comfort and pleasure, the economic and social mechanisms that aid in the manufacture and ever wider distribution of ever new inventions. Living and the standard of living are virtually synonymous, since the program in view consists not in living but in always preparing to live by always raising the standard of living. If our age is reproached with being dominantly utilitarian and materialistic, the answer is that we are *really* concerned for the "opportunity" for higher values in the future—a future that appears ever near but never nearer. An economy of abundance will for the first time in the story of man make possible the more abundant life. We still believe, if less ecstatically, in the "law of progress." Progress may be slow at times, and there may be setbacks, but the human race is marching on, with plenty of time to march. Guided by the sentimental naturalism of the eighteenth century and the utilitarian naturalism of the nineteenth, the modern world is on the right track to a paradise on earth. Those who are assailed by doubts can take refuge in the law of change, which calls for less commitment than belief in progress. The past is "the dead past." "We live in a changing world." "Change is the only constant."

It is believed, despite the fixed views and militant attitude suggested in the foregoing paragraphs, that among the prime virtues of the life intellectual is the virtue of neutrality, the impartiality we have learned from science. It is the duty of the scholar and teacher to show his exalted objectivity in all things by never taking a stand. In that case I am afraid he is not doing his duty. The neutrality so much bepraised in our universities is only a fiction. The same may be said of the insistence on relativity, the scorn of all absolutes. Professing to cast out all absolutes, to believe that all truth is purely relative to time, place, and circumstance, that it is silly to speak, for example, of "eternal values," the professor really means all absolutes save his own. His very relativity is an absolute.

It is believed that the universities, in an age of science, should be dominated throughout by scientific methods and concepts—actually, it turns out, by a distortion of scientific methods and concepts. Now, if science is above all a disinterested search for knowledge of nature, it manifestly has a large and honorable place. Yet even in the departments of natural science such a conception is often subordinated to a narrowly technological interpretation of science. And in other departments what is alleged to be scientific turns out to consist mainly of an indiscriminate transfer of scientific methods and concepts to fields of inquiry in which they are not suitable. There is usually a kind of parody involved in the application of quantitative methods, for example, to the humanities and the new social studies. It is not true that the universities *really* scientize all their subjects, though it is believed that they can and should.

It is believed, in our universities thus dedicated to science and pseudo-science, that the humanities have a significant place only insofar as they are "creative." This is the view of departments outside the humanities. As the scientist is creative in discovery and invention, so the humanist should be creative in the writing of poems and novels, the writing and production of plays and musical compositions, the making of pictures and sculpture. While the great function of science is knowledge and utility, the lesser function of literature and art is the pleasant exercise of aesthetic responses ("beauty feasts," in the phrase of Sir J. Arthur Thomson). They have nothing to do with the quest of knowledge and truth, which belongs to science alone. Criticism of literature and art is parasitic and all but futile. Indeed, the critical spirit in general (which is in fact at the heart of all the humanities, being only another term for the search for values) is a welter of subjectivity in sharp contrast to the objectivity of science. I like this, you like that; I find this true, you find that true. This makes philosophy an unreal battle of mere logic or words, a harmless pastime for those who still care for this sort of game. Theology is like philosophy, and religion is a social science. As for history, there is not much to be said for chronology, in any university subject, and, since all subjects have a history and the specialists in the various subjects are best qualified to deal with it, there is perhaps no place in a university for a department of history. The other social studies are sciences, albeit backward sciences, to be approved in proportion as they are pursued in the naturalistic spirit.

Such is the trend of opinion outside these subjects. Within the subjects is a similar distortion. Literary and artistic studies are regarded by the majority of those who engage in them as primarily historical, or even antiquarian, not creative and critical. History is largely the study of documents and the discovery and organization of facts, the massing of materials for historiography; there is scant interest in the using of the materials in the interpretative and imaginative re-creation of the past by the historian as critic and artist. In the other social studies the aim has been to proceed as scientifically as possible, regardless of the humanistic aspect of these studies, with the result that fundamental concepts and methods are in great confusion. (The same, by the way, is to be said of psychology.) Philosophy, scorned by an age of science, has sought refreshment in the methodological implications of the natural sciences and the naturalistic interpretation of current political and social movements. Religion has often been content with its new role as a social science, sometimes conceiving of campus life as a sort of laboratory.

It is believed, again, that the whole effort of the university should be directed upon the interests and problems of contemporary life. If the humanities do not play their part in this effort, so much the worse for the humanities: they will be a side show. In many quarters there is almost a hatred of the past, which is conceived as the main hindrance to progress. Its achievements are usually minimized (surely John Dewey is an improvement upon Plato), and when they are freely granted are found to be irrelevant to modern experience. Ours is a different world, the beginning of the endless age of science and democracy, the endless age of true enlightenment. It is a living world of experience, not a dead world of records and books, though, in practice, the student must be guided into it by books—our dead and deadly textbooks. The great books of the past are demonstrably full of error, and in any case do not much concern us, who are not Greeks or Elizabethans but modern Americans. If we need belles-lettres let them be not

Homer and Dante and the other classics but contemporary literature, which grows out of and reflects our environment, deals in a "meaningful" way with our problems. Human nature changes, and ours is ours. So strong is this attitude that it is tactically unwise, in many universities, to use in academic circles such words as "the past," "tradition," "heritage," "classical," "medieval," save in a tone of studied contempt.

It is believed that the university should serve the high ideal of research at the frontiers of (scientific) knowledge. Every professor should be active in original investigation and publication. His prestige depends upon this, and consequently his advancement by the administration, which especially honors outside evidence of prestige in the form of "calls." The obligation of research is accepted by most professors, though a large proportion resent the emphasis placed upon it, both those who have no talent for it and those who have the talent but are deeply interested in the liberal education of undergraduates. Teaching is relatively neglected by faculty and administration, sometimes in the comforting belief that the men who are best in research are also best in teaching. There are some qualms about the time and expense allotted to research in a people's university, so that it is given little publicity and then only in its practical or dollar-earning service to the state.

It is believed—despite the notion that research should animate the state university with a high ideal—that a high ideal is *not* suitable in a state university. A state university is a people's university, of the people, for the people, and, in the end, by the people. It must offer them what they spontaneously want, or what they are supposed to want, not what they need and might be taught to want. Of course it is hard to say what they need, or even what they want, but as a working hypothesis we will assume that they want what is useful and practical, not in a remote and indirect way but immediately, something tangibly marketable. To attempt to stuff culture down the throats of *hoi polloi*, to aim at changing raw youth into well-rounded men and women, would be at the least inappropriate. The published catalogue should doubtless state some such general objective, since everyone wishes to be well-rounded, but the curriculum, teaching methods, and adviser system, it should be understood, will be based on the realities of the situation. A faculty of utilitarian specialists, having no horror of one-sidedness, will know how to change raw youth into utilitarian specialists.

It is believed, more specifically, that what the people of the state want is a job-centered education. Frankly, this is what our "student-centered" education comes to. We must prepare the students, who are also people of the state, for employment in a vocation and pecuniary advantage over the unprepared. We must open opportunity to them through a generous variety of curricula, adding one program after another according to a demand imagined if not real. We must include training not only for the professions but also for many lesser vocations among the more than 25,000 recognized by the national census. We need not be deterred by snobbish distinctions between dignified and humble vocations, nor between "education" and "training." Train we must, if our students are to land jobs and hold them. To some extent we must also train them for other "adult activities" and "life situations," such as disease prevention, marriage, and leisure, indeed for a "total adjustment" to contemporary society. To the fact that no one can say what life will be like during the half century our students will span after they leave us, we regretfully close our eyes. To the fact that about half of our students never graduate, and that of those who do half either do not pursue their chosen vocation for more than three or four years or do not pursue it at all, we regretfully close our eyes. We are doing the best we can under such circumstances.

It is believed that the foundations of education, which are biological and psychological, lie in motivation and individual differences. The strongest motive is vocational; the student's desire to enter a freely chosen kind of work provides the motive that enables him to study with the maximum interest and profit. Many students are happily "self-motivated," know at the start what they want to prepare for. The rest "find themselves" more or less slowly or not at all. It is the business of the personnel service and the faculty to prod them into finding themselves, that is, into learning what occupational groove they could be made to fit, what sort of tool they were created to be. It may be noted in passing that to fit men into vocational groupings is a strange way to recognize their *individual* differences. Yet all the faculty talk is of individual differences. The old declaration of independence, which affirmed the half-truth that men are created equal, has been supplanted by the new declaration, which affirms the half-truth that they are created unique. A leading psychologist who pushes the concept of differences to the extreme has ridiculed the liberal and social view of education by saying, "Where the Great Maker created all human beings different, it is the function of the teacher to make them all alike." Apparently the psychologist would have this read: "Where the Great Maker created all human beings different, it is the function of the teacher to make them as different as possible." Another reading, quite out of favor, is to the effect that all men are at once the same and different, and that liberal and social education should develop their samenesses, leaving the differences mainly to special education.

It is believed that no common knowledge may be regarded as essential. The uniform requirement of any particular subject would not be in harmony with the concepts of motivation and individual differences. Besides, there is no specific knowledge agreed upon which every educated person must acquire, and even if he acquired such knowledge he would forget it before or soon after graduation. And what department dare assert that all students should be required to take a course in that department, unless it is prepared to grant the same privilege to every other department? From this political situation two or three required courses may, in practice, emerge, since some departments are strong through numbers, through leadership, or merely customary recognition, and furthermore some subjects do seem to be very important if not altogether essential. The general opinion remains, however, that prescription is psychologically unsound and perhaps undemocratic as well. Subjects, if not men, were created free and equal.

It is believed that knowledge is not its own end but merely a means, an instrument for use, and that the use contemplated in education should be the development of abilities. Apparently the assumption is made (without justification) that abilities learned in college will last, while knowledge will not. Abilities do not involve prescription, since they can be learned in any subject. Thus, the ability to use scientific method may be acquired in physical education, the ability to perceive aesthetic properties may be acquired in mathematics, etc. Or, to shift the point of view to the teacher, any subject, whether Latin or radio broadcasting, may be taught liberally or narrowly, according to the kind and range of abilities that are promoted. The old theory that abilities may be "transferred" from one field to another has been exploded. To be sure, transfer is possible under favorable conditions, when the student or the teacher or both seek to establish relations between subjects and progressively integrate the abilities learned. But apparently we are not to assume or assure these favorable conditions.

It is believed, in view of the preceding doctrines, that a student-centered college must provide the "tailor-made curriculum," that is, a different curriculum for each student. Faculty regulations concerning courses should have great flexibility. This does not argue a return to an unlimited elective system and its attendant chaos. There should be a "core" of courses required in the three great divisions of learning, the natural sciences, the social sciences, and the humanities, permitting, however, "options" within these divisions. And the core should be kept as small as possible, between say twenty-four and thirty-four semester hours. In addition to all options within the core, the entire remaining program of eighty-six to ninety-six hours should be open to selection according to individual differences in aptitude and interest. Who is to do all the opting and selecting? The individual student? the Greek letter houses and the dormitories? the parents? the faculty adviser? Although no system based on any of these sources of wisdom has worked well, a system of faculty advising is usually relied on: the cause of liberal education is entrusted to the specialist. He will know the student and know what is good for him. If persuasion is too time-consuming or ineffective, he will have recourse to "strong talk across the desk" (or else surrender his responsibility to the student). Since the "uneducated specialists," as Mr. Hutchins terms them, have their individual differences and not always the purest motivation, we again face chaos. And chaos will have to be accepted, unless we are prepared to have advisers for the advisers—presumably the administration. In this case the faculty will surrender its responsibility to the dean, or master-tailor.

4. EDUCATIONISTS

Such is the naturalistic conception of life and of education widely prevalent in state universities and many other institutions as well. Most of it reads curiously like a summary of the notions associated with teachers' colleges and with departments, schools, and colleges of education within the universities. In truth there is no great gap between the mentality of professors of "subjects" and professors of "Education." (The conventional terms are unfair, since education is also a subject and a better one than many another.) The naturalistic interpretation of man leads logically to a naturalistic theory of education agreeable alike to both groups. Professors of the various subjects have been deeply indebted to the same line of thought as that which the educationists have used, a line that runs through such men as Bacon, Rousseau, Darwin, Spencer, and Dewey. They may not know but would read with sympathy the works of the successors of John Dewey, men like William H. Kilpatrick, who aimed to establish a science of education, beginning with a dissertation on "Animal Intelligence," and Harold Rugg, author of *The Child-Centered School*. The most vital bond between the two groups is perhaps that of modern psychology, which both have applied in a spirit more zealous than critical.

In view of this close kinship, it is at first glance surprising that professors of subjects, along with a few professors of Education, look upon educationists as a whole with disdain and hostility. For this attitude there are several main reasons. One lies in the conflict between concern for "content" and concern for "method," that is, the belief of professors of subjects that prospective teachers must know as thoroughly as possible the subjects they are to teach, and the belief of professors of Education that teachers must learn how to teach and must therefore include in their preparation a considerable amount of Education. This conflict is heightened by the observation that the science of Education is not yet impressive, that professors of Education are not themselves superior teachers (though one would expect men in "professional education" to surpass those engaged in amateur education), that students required to take courses in Education show, despite vocational motivation, so little of that interest which is held to be requisite, and that the results of the many hours taken in Education are so disappointing when tested by actual practice in the schools.

A second reason for hostility is the belief of professors of subjects that professors of Education have indulged in a bewildering succession of fads. This general opinion is shared, here and there, by prominent professors of Education, such as Edgar W. Knight and I. L. Kandel. As the latter has put it in an article on "The Fantasia of Current Education," "Ever since some educational theorists made the profound discovery that we live in a changing world, that authoritarianism began to be undermined by Galileo and that life is precarious and the future uncertain, experimentalism has run riot and education has been bombarded with a chaotic welter of theories." This welter has characterized the Progressive Education fathered by John Dewey, a contemporary application of the ancient Sophistical rejection of all permanent values and all tradition. Among the advocates of Progressive Education have been both moderates and radicals. Many university professors of subjects, moderates without knowing it, associate the movement with radicals who have reduced its half-truths to quarter-truths and made them ridiculous.

Finally, the hostility is more and more due to fear of the power educationists are already exerting and may exert disastrously in the future. Primary and secondary schools are securely in their control, owing largely to the political protection they have built up, and colleges and universities are increasingly feeling their influence. Faculties of higher education, engrossed in subjects and in the promotion of departmental interests, are in danger of losing by default the battle for control of educational policy. They have in their midst a large group, the professors of Education, who devote full time to the advancement of their cause. When the war came, and with it an inevitable tendency to regimentation directed from Washington, the education experts were naturally in request, and the academic hostility toward them grew. It was not only academic. Writing in *Harper's*, Bernard DeVoto, for example, espoused the cause of the scholars and teachers, who feared that "the accident of war has delivered teaching and scholarship into the hands of their mortal enemies." The professional educationists, he said, "have the charts, the graphs, the gadgets, and the pretty machines, the programs and gospels and theories, the pretentious and half-lunatic philosophies which will convince Congress (as they have always convinced legislatures).... The future of higher education in America will be at the mercy of the Teachers College mind."

A similar alarm was voiced by Dean William C. DeVane of Yale. What have the secondary schools, under the leadership of teachers' colleges, actually accomplished? The high school pupils graduate "unable to write, read, or speak English; unable to cope with mathematical problems which require algebra and trigonometry in a time when we are in dire need of these commodities; unable to read or speak fluently any foreign language in a time when to be provincial is to be only partially alive; unable to remember, much less to understand, a few facts about the history of their country; unable to think clearly, and too undisciplined to behave considerately; ungrounded in the intellectual virtues." What, then, would happen if the Federal government gave the professional educationists an equivalent opportunity in the colleges and universities? "The government would put our institutions into the hand of political-minded professors of education and educational bureaucrats, and that would reduce higher education to a mediocrity which it has not yet reached in America."

Even if the fear of Federal control turns out to be exaggerated or baseless, the fear of educationist control will remain. And not without reason. If all knowledge is the province of the subject faculties, all education would seem to be the province of the Education faculty. As experts in a new science inspired by an age of science, as supporters of the philosophy of democracy which they conceive to have been the gift of John Dewey to the world, the educationists naturally regard themselves as destined to shape higher education as they have shaped the schools below. There need be no sudden change. The state university of today largely conforms to their views; the state university of tomorrow may conform wholly. The danger is real. Yet signs are not wanting, as Leonard Carmichael admitted in his inaugural address at Tufts a year before the war, that "the naturalistic tradition of American education" has been "shaken almost in its day of victory." When the war came it was shaken violently.

5. New Forces

"The twentieth century was cradled in great, not to say stupendous hopes—hopes as to man, as to history, as to the universe itself. Whereas the old-fashioned religion had taught that 'there is no health in us,' that human nature is evil, even sinful, and has to be crushed, we, of the twentieth century, have believed in human nature, holding it to be essentially sound. So much so, in fact, that we have used human nature as our norm and have defined the highest good as the satisfaction of human needs. We have looked to no far-off Kingdom of Heaven, but to the cure of human evils on this earth. And we have believed such a cure to be concretely attainable. Enlighten the mind, spread education through all the classes of society, conquer disease, overcome poverty by a reform of economic institutions, raise the standard of living by the application of science to human needs, advance the front of democracy—has not this been the program of liberalism everywhere? Along with this faith in human nature has gone a belief in a universal law of progress—that somehow humanity is irresistibly marching to its goal and that the very cosmos is conspiring for its success. The faith in progress was really no part of the new scientific mentality—indeed it was hostile to it, being a relic of deism; but still there it was radiating a glow of hope upon the human scene. We were not only confident; we were complacent and arrogant, feeling ourselves Promethean rebels, conquerors both of nature and of the gods.

"But now something has happened—a halt has been called; the two wars—or rather the one war in its two phases—with their attendant economic disasters and political chaos, have shattered our simple faith. Our optimism is proved to have been not only shallow but false. Human nature has disclosed unsuspected depths of irrationality, brutality and barbarism; history is not an upward-onward march. Obviously something is very wrong with human nature and with the nature of things."

These are the words of Raphael Demos in his sober review of Niebuhr which appeared in the *New Republic* (of all places!) in 1943. The new mood here described, the growing suspicion that our optimism has been sentimental and unrealistic, has not yet fundamentally altered the public mind, at least in America; still less has it disturbed the great majority of comfortable intellectuals in our universities. Whether the new mood will become affirmative and will serve as the starting-point for a humanistic revival, depends largely on the political prospects opened by the peace. Yet in any case there are forces, both without and within the universities, which offer some hope for the future of the humanistic spirit in American civilization and hence in American state universities.

There is in our society an increasing disillusionment with the results of naturalism. Many persons have abandoned the naïve optimism inherited from the last two centuries and at the same time are resolved not to succumb to the merely negative disillusionment that paralyzed mind and will after the last war. They perceive that democracy is neither a panacea nor a mistake but a great hope demanding great effort. They perceive that science as a priceless means of attaining knowledge and organizing effort cannot itself provide the ends toward which effort should be directed. They perceive, in particular, that the gifts of technology are only instruments of living and leave untouched the problem of what to live for. They are aware of a vast imbalance, in our type of civilization, of the elements that seem necessary in life, an imbalance which strikes them most forcibly as one between man's tremendous capacity for controlling nature and his tremendous incapacity for controlling himself. They reflect upon the imbalance, again, between the hope that materialistic humanitarianism would give a basis for the good life and the bleak and stubborn failure of the good life to rise spontaneously on this foundation. They see, above all, that naturalism, having broken down the old faith of the Occident, is now losing confidence in its ability to offer a substitute that can cope with the realities of experience. As Geoffrey Crowther, editor of *The Economist,* has put it: "The western democratic world is perilously close to a vacuum of faith.... But the trouble about a vacuum is that it gets filled, and if there are no angels available to fill it, fools—or worse—rush in." We have seen them rush.

There is an increasing perception that without faith the modern world will never solve its mundane problems, and that the quest of faith must mean, first of all, a revival of belief in values, the special province of the humanities. More and more this has been the burden of forthright statements by men in varied fields of thought and action.

For example, in the words of Edward Hallett Carr, professor of politics, "The esential nature of the crisis through which we are living is neither military, nor political, nor economic, but moral. A new faith in a new moral purpose is required to reanimate our political and economic system." Almost the same words have been used by Theodore M. Greene, professor of philosophy, who finds the crisis to be not military, nor political, nor economic, but in the stratum beneath these, "the stratum of cultural values and modes of thought," and beneath this again the level of "spiritual commitment and religious faith," and who concludes that "the humanities, having to do so essentially with man's cultural and spiritual life, should make, and can make, and must make a unique contribution to our national welfare." Or, as Raymond B. Fosdick, president of the Rockefeller Foundation, puts it: "Particularly must we rely on the humanists—the historians, the philosophers, the artists, the poets, the novelists, the dramatists—all those who fashion ideas, concepts, and forms that give meaning and value to life and furnish the patterns of conduct." And again, President Seymour, historian, along with the Corporation of Yale University, issued a statement warning of the "impoverishment of the nation's mind and soul" and called for concern, even during the war, with "the less tangible values of our culture." President Conant, less fearful of the neglect of humanistic studies during the war, predicted for them a new period of growth after the war. Boldly sustaining "the thesis that universities are concerned fundamentally with the eternal verities," that theirs is "the guardianship of eternal values," he held that "a general education must be based on a study of the arts, letters, and the various aspects of philosophy," since "in these fields of study, and in these only, the true nature of the exercise of a free choice of values by a civilized man can be understood." Lawyer and political leader, the late Wendell L. Willkie, in one of the best educational addresses of recent years, justified the humanities in terms of democracy—the equality of minds enfranchised. "When you range back and forth through the centuries, when you weigh the utterance of some great thinker or absorb the meaning of some great composition, in painting or music or poetry; when you live these things within yourself and measure yourself against them—only then do you become an initiate in the world of the free. It is in the liberal arts that you acquire the ability to make a truly free and individual choice."

Opinions of this sort, rare a decade ago, have in the last years multiplied. They acquire a special significance when held by natural scientists. It used to be the habit of many scientists to assume (not of course as scientists but as naturalistic philosophers) that science is about all that mankind needs, that its abstractions cover all of reality that is of real concern for man, that its method is competent ultimately to solve the problems of the good life, and that philosophy and religion have been mostly wishful thinking, private or social dreams. Today this uncritical scientism is rapidly declining. I have already quoted a distinguished chemist who speaks of eternal values, and who holds that general education should be based not on science but on the humanities. Let me add the views of some biologists and physicists.

Sir J. Arthur Thomson has clearly stated the limited enterprise of science. "Science," he says, "is a particular way of looking at the world, but it is not the only way.... We learn by feeling and living as well as by scientifically knowing. Science is one of the pathways toward the truth, but there are other pathways. *Vivendo discimus*. By certain methods, determinedly abstract and partial, methods of weighing and measuring, analyzing and reducing, science formulates the fractions of reality which it grips. But by hypotheses it only gets at fractions of reality, since it is too daring a postulate to suppose that scientific methods are always able to exhaust the manifoldness of a situation." Science leaves wide open, for others than scientists, the entire range of human ends. "It is impossible for us," says Robert A. Millikan, "to get along without the aid of certain people who can be trusted to speak with authority on the vitally important questions of human ends. The scientist provides us with extensive enough information regarding what *is*, but unless we have those among us to tell us also *what makes for*, and what does not make for, our more fundamental well-being, we are lost." That we are indeed lost is suggested by Albert Einstein, who remarks that whatever scientific method in the hand of man will produce "depends entirely on the nature of the aims alive in mankind. Once these aims exist, the scientific method furnishes means to realize them. But it cannot furnish the aims themselves. The scientific method itself would not have led to anything, it would not even have been born at all without a passionate striving for clear understanding. Perfection of means and confusion of aims seem, in my opinion, to characterize our age."

Thus in field after field, and by men of the most varied mentality, the humanistic spirit has spoken, in America as abroad, against the intellectual bewilderment and spiritual apathy of the twentieth century. "On every hand today—in the press, the radio, the school—we are called upon to defend 'the Humanities,' the more human arts and human values, against war abroad and against socio-economic and scientific-naturalistic fatalism at home." This observation by Lennox Grey of Teachers College, Columbia (in his editorial foreword to an "impartial" thesis on *The Revival of the Humanities in American Education*) will serve to remind us that the only group who, when called upon to "defend 'the Humanities,'" have failed to respond to the call are the faculties and administration of the teachers' colleges of America.

As for the public at large, a significant portion of it is aware of the essential aimlessness of modern living and is looking round for guidance. It is responsive to newspaper columnists who unjustly berate science and economics for taking us on "The Ride to Nowhere" and who offer philosophy or the great books of the past as better approaches to happiness. It has shown itself ready for a book on liberal education written in the humanistic spirit, a book by Mark Van Doren which went through several printings in rapid succession. It is prepared to listen to the view that vocations were made for man, not man for vocations, that the education called Progressive was really digressive, and that if we learn by doing we also learn by being done. You cannot fool all of the people all of the time. There is in the public a sense of humor, the corrective and sanative aspect of the humanistic spirit, which manifests itself negatively as a kind of skepticism and positively as a desire for proportion. It rises to clearness in our cartoonists and our homespun philosophers (like Will Rogers), not in our university specialists, who are strangers to the comic spirit of Erasmus.

In terms of ideas, perhaps the best hope for a revival of the humanities lies in a conception which has in recent years appealed both to intellectuals, such as those I have quoted, and to much of the public. It is the dignity of man. The phrase is rarely defined, in modern or any other terms. It conveys a vague affirmation that man, whatever his beastliness, possesses some inherent excellence or nobleness. When some effort is made at analysis, man's dignity is likely to be found in his freedom, though what is meant is rather liberty, the absence of outer constraint. Thus, the dignity of man is violated by any form of exploitation, bodily or mental. According to Bruce Bliven, of the *New Republic,* "The conception of the dignity of the individual, of freedom and fairness for all, is a startlingly new one." This amazing remark suggests how completely the naturalist mind, immersed in the contemporaneous and obliged to discover everything for the first time, has broken with the traditions of civilization. As all educated persons know, the conception of the dignity of the individual goes back through the entire history of America to the heritage which Europe received from its cultural foundations in Greece and Judea. Only in comparatively recent times has the conception become vague. In its present form it has little potency. In proportion as this is recognized, we shall doubtless witness efforts to infuse into it some degree of dynamic meaning. Those who have broken with the traditions of civilization will sooner or later wish to find a new reason, perhaps a "startlingly" new reason, for believing in the dignity of man. If the effort is honest, it will merit encouragement, not scorn. Meanwhile we shall do well, surely, to revitalize the old conceptions of human dignity which are at the very foundations of our civilization and its democratic institutions.

It is increasingly recognized that this task, while it concerns the whole of our society, is a special obligation of our intellectuals. Our academic intellectuals, under the pressure of a crisis growing more and more acute, are aware that a humanistic reorientation of the higher learning calls for the united efforts of entire university faculties. At Princeton, for example, a group of eight distinguished professors representing astronomy, chemistry, economics, history, classics, philosophy, and religion collaborated in a statement presented at the 1941 meeting of the Conference on Science, Philosophy, and Religion held at Columbia University. That the opinions I have expressed are nowise novel, but representative of a trend, may be suggested by a series of quotations which may serve as a summary of the argument I have so far advanced:

"Democratic institutions and cultural activities rest upon the assumption that man, while a part of nature, is a spiritual being. . . .

"Spiritual life and its laws . . . are not identical with any of the phenomena of laws of nature described by the natural sciences; and whatever description of them the natural sciences may be capable of giving cannot affect their reality and their values.

"The human spirit, of course, is dependent to an undetermined extent upon the natural processes of the body and its environment. But, though it is thus conditioned by biological and physical processes it cannot be identified with them and can be fully understood only by means of distinctive methods and categories suitable to its distinctive nature. . . .

"The capacity of man to relate himself to an ultimate source of meaning and worth and to value things and persons for their intrinsic worth is thus essential to a true conception of the human spirit. There have been, however, different ideas about the ultimate source of meaning and worth and the practical implications of man's relation to it. The two major conceptions of the spiritual life which have dominated Western thought are the intellectual and contemplative conception derived primarily from the Greeks and the Hebraic-Christian moral and religious conception. . . .

"Naturalism denies both man's relation to an order of ultimate values and his dependence upon a cosmic spiritual Power. It thus divorces him from the moral and spiritual order to which he belongs and upon which he depends for strength and direction. . . .

"Many who hold to this naturalistic view in democratic countries are unaware of the dangers in their position. . . . They act as if they still believed in the spiritual conception of man which they have intellectually repudiated. They try to maintain their feeling for the dignity of man, while paying homage to an essentially materialistic philosophy according to which man is simply a highly developed animal. They are loyal to their democratic society and culture, but by their theory they deny the spiritual nature of man and his values upon which it has been built. In short, they are living off the spiritual capital which has come down to them from their classical and religious heritage, while at the same time they ignore that heritage itself as antiquated and false.

"Since this contradiction will prove to be intellectually intolerable, scholars and teachers must recover and reaffirm the spiritual conception of man and his good which we have derived from Greek and Hebraic-Christian sources. If they fail to do this, not only religious reverence and moral responsibility, but also the scholarly activities with which they are directly concerned, will be gravely endangered. Already, under totalitarian regimes, and to a lesser extent in the democracies, these activities are being undermined."

6. The Heritage of Free Men

Our Occidental civilization derives its strength ultimately from the Great Tradition, which is the conflux of our humanistic legacy from the pagan world and our religious legacy from Judaism and Christianity. This twofold tradition may be approached in terms of American experience. In the seventeenth century we had in America an inadequate Christianity, in the eighteenth century an inadequate classicism; only in the late nineteenth century did a corrosive naturalism finally give us our vacuum of faith. If today educators would concern themselves with values, they must begin by acquainting the youth of America with the values which America has shared with the rest of the Occident. This is not a proposal for turning back the clock, for trying to go back to the Middle Ages or Greek antiquity, for attempting to confine the human spirit. It is a proposal of an emancipation from the provincial dogmas of the day, and from all the forms of indoctrination and regimentation which threaten to bedevil our education. To avoid these dangers the best way, in the end, is to give students access to their essential heritage. Burn the books (or ignore them, which is the same) if you would make slaves. "Open the books," as Willkie said, "if you wish to be free" and to make free men.

The books opened most often by Thomas Jefferson, who

assuredly had no desire to turn the clock back, were not contemporary works, though he knew these too, but the classics of Greece and Rome. "By a strange anomaly," as Professor Chinard observes, "the son of a pioneer, the young man supposedly brought up under frontier influences, felt more kinship with Greece and republican Rome than with the philosophies of London, Paris, or Geneva." He preferred to read Homer, Epictetus, Cicero, Tacitus, and he read them not merely for aesthetic satisfaction but rather for knowledge of man and society. When vice-president of the United States, he testified that "to read the Latin and Greek authors in their original is a sublime luxury.... I thank on my knees Him who directed my early education, for having put into my possession this rich source of delight; and I would not exchange it for anything which I could then have acquired, and have not since acquired." Jefferson was not alone in having occasion to thank Him—and those—who directed his early education, as James J. Walsh made clear in his book on the education of the Founding Fathers. They were disciplined in the arts of free men and possessed the knowledge most useful in establishing the institutions of free men, whereas their descendants in our time, as Walter Lippmann and the late Walter A. Jessup have argued, are ceasing to be free because they have lost the discipline and knowledge of their great tradition. If we are to return to the tradition, we shall have to do so mainly through translations. As readers of Greek and Latin know, this will entail a serious loss. Yet the power of great books is so strong even at second hand that translations have again and again proved a fructifying and dynamic agency in the development of national cultures in Italy, France, Germany, and England.

The great tradition is Christian as well as classical. A deist, not a Christian in any orthodox sense, Jefferson had pondered earnestly, as perhaps few of our political leaders have done in recent years, the doctrine of Jesus, as well as other religions and philosophies which have had an important history. But another American president, Abraham Lincoln, serves as a better symbol of the sustaining and ennobling power of Christianity. It is true that he too held aloof from orthodox creeds.

Yet he read the Bible as few read it today, and found in it patterns of what life should be, of what life would be so far as he could guide its course for himself and his people. He learned to feel and speak like the authors of the Bible and the Book of Common Prayer. He was our foremost Christian president. If government by the people is not to perish from the earth, it can ill afford to base its concept of human dignity on anything less than a religious sense of the spiritual worth of each person, as opposed to the naturalistic view of the individual as a mere social unit. The inhumanity of the fascist tyranny brought this home, for example, to a novelist who had won his reputation in the school of naturalism—Thomas Mann. Democracy and Christianity, as he declared in an address at Hobart College, "are united to such an extent that democracy may be called the political expression of our Christian feeling for life, of Christianity on earth. And we may conclude from the close relationship of democracy and Christianity, not that they will disappear together, but that they will survive together." If this is true, effort will be needed to restore the vitality of the Christian faith, and in this effort higher education must have a role. Experience has shown that it is possible to have a school of religion even within a state university. Without such a school it is still possible to present in the course of study the history of Christianity, and to include much of the King James Bible in the reading of every student, if only because this translation is one of the masterpieces of English literature.

Open the books if you wish to be free, above all the books central in Occidental civilization. Democracies have at last begun to realize what is at stake, says I. L. Kandel in *The End of an Era*, and they will maintain themselves only by continuing "the heritage of Athens and Jerusalem, whose possession made men free." This is a large task for secondary and higher education in the humanities. Yet circumstances may soon force us to be concerned with Oriental civilization as well, with at least some knowledge of the history and tradition of China and India. What is most modern in these countries is Occidental (a mixed blessing!) and familiar enough to us. But their national cultures are powerfully shaped by the past, resembling in many ways in China the humanism, and in India the religion, of the West. Confucius and Buddha will take on a new importance for us if the tradition of civilization is to be seen, in the phrase of Ordway Tead, "universally and not merely occidentally." Nor can we rest content here. Outside the central stream of the humanistic and religious tradition are many Western works which have so profoundly affected the course of civilization that they might well have a place in the course of study, the works of men like Machiavelli, Rousseau, Darwin, Marx, Nietzsche. They must be represented not only because of their historic importance but for reasons even more compelling: because they will protect us against too firm and assured guidance of the young, and because the young have a right to access to greatness of whatever kind. We shall keep *all* the books open.

7. Liberal Education

An education inspired by the humanistic ideal will be a liberal education. It alone is fully worthy of the dignity of man. Its object is clear: to liberate the young from ignorance, prejudice, foolishness, and the like; to aid them to attain freedom through realization of their capacities as men and women. An education aiming at something less than the human is in so far barbarous, for example the slavish education of the totalitarian state, or a vocational education which degrades men to tools. To be sure, men must have vocations, and therefore preparation ranging from a few weeks or months to a term of years, according to the calling selected, but such preparation, whether narrowly or broadly conceived, is not what we mean by liberal education.

When liberal education arose in ancient Greece, it was the discipline of free men—the unfree learned the vocations. Today the division is not between classes but within the individual. To make a living he works forty hours a week, more or less; to live he has all the rest, to live freely, as he chooses. Only a relatively few men can have vocations that exercise their full humanity. The vast majority can feel free only in their free time, and they want more and more free time. Whatever the value of their vocational work to themselves and to the state, the value of their free time is even greater both to themselves and to the state as well. For the state needs citizens even more than it needs shopkeepers, carpenters, bankers, lawyers, needs men who are more than instruments in the work of the world, who experience life in many ways, develop many interests, play a role in the formation of that public opinion which is the real government of the democratic state, and attain a morale high enough to sustain the state in peace and war. The most civilized state will, if resources and manpower are equal, be the strongest, happiest, and most memorable.

From the point of view of the American state, therefore, the function of liberal education, as President Roosevelt said at Jefferson's alma mater, is that of "training men for citizenship in a great republic." "This," he went on to say, "was in the spirit of the old America, and it is, I believe, in the spirit of the America of today. The necessities of our time demand that men avoid being set in grooves, that they avoid the occupational predestination of the older world.... Every form of cooperative human endeavor cries out for men and women who, in their thinking processes, will know something of the broader aspects of any given problem." Clearly, the states of the Union cannot afford, in their public universities, the multiplication of occupational curricula that offer what Edmund Burke somewhere calls "tricking short-cuts and little fallacious facilities." Even in the professions liberal training is gravely hindered by the motivation of the student, who, as another of our presidents—Woodrow Wilson—put it, "will be immersed in the things that touch his profit and loss, and a man is not free to think inside that territory."

Liberal education is one thing and vocational education another, and no amount of sophistry about liberal education "in a new sense of the term" will alter the fact. That they differ in principle has been recognized from ancient times to the present. As they were apart in ancient Greece, so they were in the Middle Ages, when an education in the seven liberal arts was prescribed for every student before he turned to his professional preparation. They were apart again in the Renaissance. In the Mantuan school of Vittorino, for instance, which merits a few words here because it blended so well the classical and Christian traditions, the aim, as stated by W. H. Woodward, was "to lay foundations in liberal culture to serve as the necessary preliminaries to specific training for careers." As a humanist educator, Vittorino da Feltre sought to create "the complete citizen," or, to say the same thing another way, "to secure the harmonious development of mind, body, and character." The curriculum was limited by the meagre scientific knowledge then available, but it supplemented the humanities with mathematics and some natural science (astrology was discarded for astronomy). Ancient culture was not pursued in abstraction but focused earnestly on the needs of the present. As for individual differences, Vittorino considered, "almost with reverence, the tastes and bent of each of his pupils." Before going on to professional study his pupils stayed with him "until they had passed their twenty-first year." On the whole, his school might well serve as a fruitful source of suggestion for the liberal college in modern America, as it has served for secondary education in modern Europe. Our high schools accomplish something in liberal education and could accomplish more, but under our system it is the responsibility of the college to complete the program, postponing occupational training till it *has* been completed—if necessary till the student has passed his twenty-first year.

But the beguiling hope persists: Could not liberal education be attempted *through* vocational education? Many persons, like John Dewey in his article in *Fortune* in 1944, have argued that liberal education as we have known it from ancient till recent times is a relic of the pre-democratic and pre-scientific past, and that today the appropriate education must be technical and vocational. It is frankly admitted that our job-centered training has been too narrow and mechanical. So we should set about "liberalizing our technical and vocational education." How this is to be done has not been made very clear. One might suppose, to take a concrete example, that a course in

Advanced Clothing would be so taught as to lead the student back to earlier conceptions of costume, eventually to Greek costume and hence to Greek art and hence to the whole Greek view of life, perhaps attracting the student to an elective in ancient civilization which he would "feed into" his vocational preparation. But this is not what Dr. Dewey means. His great object is to make the student modern, that is, scientific. The past, lingering in our conceptions and standards, is only a clog that prevents our going forward with undivided zeal toward "the scientific way of life." Vocational education must be liberalized by showing how modern industry rests on scientific processes. What this would seem to mean, in our course on Advanced Clothing, is that the student would be brought to "awareness of the scientific processes embodied" in designing, constructing, and preserving clothing and in relating contemporary clothing to contemporary social forces. Whatever it means the net result might be the improvement of vocational education but could not be the improvement of liberal education.

If liberal education is not concerned with vocational skills, it is profoundly concerned with other skills and abilities. There are many things which the student, as a human being, should be able to do. He should be able to care for his body, his physical welfare. He should be able to speak, to read, to write, on a plane suited to his college years and later life. He should know how to think: how to think in the concrete terms of science, how to think in the abstract manner of mathematics and philosophy, and how to think (and feel and will) in the humanistic realm of value-judgments. He should be able to relate his growing abilities and knowledge in the gradual development of a philosophy of life to which he is willing provisionally to commit himself. He should be able to relate his developing philosophy to active experience in living, to complete the revolving circle of thought and action. Through the discipline of his entire nature he will come into ever fuller possession of himself as a human being and as a particular person.

Something like this set of skills and abilities is agreed upon by virtually all who profess belief in liberal education. The list may never be altogether the same, and differences in emphasis will appear, but on the whole the objectives are sufficiently agreed upon. There is a fundamental cleavage, however, between those who assert that liberal education is concerned only with abilities and those who assert that it involves both abilities and knowledge.

The tendency has been especially marked among educationists to limit the objectives to abilities, using knowledge only as means. What sort of person, they ask, do we want the student to be when we are through with him? What do we want to have happen to him in consequence of his education? Once we have decided upon the end-product, it will be easy to plan a curriculum and hire and fire teachers according to their success in changing the student as we want him changed. The student is to be conditioned, the teacher is to be approved or purged. This totalitarian parody of liberal education—I have stated it crudely because I have heard it stated crudely—shows some signs of becoming a menace in a society floundering for lack of assured values. America today has more reason than England had in 1935 to heed the warning then sounded by John Murray, principal of University College, Exeter. "Any dictator," he cried, "might see his chance in the present state of the universities that have sold themselves to utility. If the universities have lost their humanism, or the prophetic and magisterial tones in preaching it, need a dictator hesitate? From him that hath not shall be taken away even that which he hath."

Protection against this perversion is offered by those who assert that liberal education involves not only abilities but common knowledge, common knowledge not of anything at random but of the liberating best that man has said and done. Even if the goal were allowed to be abilities alone, it could be attained most effectively by the use of the best materials. After all is anyone so crass as to maintain that the history of Peru would do as well as the history of modern Europe, the literature of the Philippines as well as the literature of England, an African dialect as well as French, the science of numismatics as well as the science of biology? The knowledge to be learned may obviously be more or less relevant. Is there, then, a most relevant knowledge? Is there an indispensable best? If so, who shall say what it is? At this point the specialist professor will break down in utter helplessness. But even he, if he could drop his pose or his politics, would quickly begin a list of essentials, or of things so important that they might as well be called essentials. There is a large area of general agreement as to the best that man has said and done, large enough for the planning of a curriculum. This best will guard the student against conditioning to the intellectual fashions and veering passions of the day, fashions and passions to which the faculty itself is not immune. He will have at hand a standard by which to measure the instruction he is receiving. Even if the knowledge opened to him is not necessarily the best, it will have high value as common knowledge, shared knowledge, tending to unite his and other students' minds in common experience, common duties, common memories. Liberal education based on common knowledge is social education; vocational education separating youth into groups according to special interests is unsocial education.

When a common fund of knowledge has been selected, the liberal college will begin to take on a definiteness of type comparable to that of the professional schools. Once this definiteness of type has been fully established in terms of objectives, curriculum, and teaching methods, the uniform requirement of specific knowledge will seem no more arbitrary than it does today in training for the professions. If something like half of the total Bachelor's program is made common, the other half will be available for election among advanced liberal studies, or for concentration upon a segment of the field of learning, to be chosen according to individual differences in interest and ability and to be studied in the same liberal manner.

8. The Great Curriculum

What should the common studies be? In a humanistic reorientation, it goes without saying, the humanities will take on a new importance. But can we be satisfied with the thesis of President Conant that a general education must be based on literature, the arts, and philosophy, even if we add history, which he has elsewhere predicted will be the most widely required study in the next fifty years? All these are humanities; is the humanistic spirit content to ignore science? The answer must be clear and unequivocal.

Historically, the answer is plain: an education permeated with the humanistic spirit has always included science. In ancient Greece, science—mathematics, astronomy, some natural history—was a part of liberal education. In the Renaissance, in the school of Vittorino, for example, it was likewise included. That science was sometimes disparaged by the humanists of the Renaissance is not surprising, in view of the scant knowledge of nature then existing. Science was little more than a promise or a hope, while the humanities had attained a dazzling achievement as far back as the fifth century B.C., indeed still earlier in the greatest of all poets, Homer. By the late nineteenth century this contrast had disappeared: science had arrived, it too had attained a dazzling achievement, and it claimed and won its place in education. If the zeal of its opponents was occasionally excessive, so was the zeal of its proponents. One must regret the mutual hostility of the two sides that attended the arrival of science in education and that lingers with us to this day, because it was not and is not justified.

The hostility is the result of mistaken attitudes. On the one side, scientists have often depreciated the humanities as not concerned with knowledge, on the assumption that there is only one kind of knowledge, scientific knowledge. They have believed that science is competent, and alone competent, to deal securely and fruitfully with everything natural and human. All fields of knowledge should be freed of unvalidated guesses, armchair philosophizing, the drag of superstition, and be duly scientized. "What knowledge is of most worth?" "The answer is always—Science." This attitude, as I have already suggested, comes not from science but from philosophy, the philosophy of naturalism. On the other side: humanists have often depreciated the sciences as materialistic, as if they were responsible for the sordid world of the machine, of big business and little living, a world in which things are in the saddle and ride mankind. When this has been their attitude, humanists have forgotten that the source of what they term materialism is, as Michael Pupin rightly declared, not in "any material structure raised by the genius of man," but "in the deepest depths of the human soul where selfishness and greed, hatred and fear" have displaced "beauty and goodness." The evil from which we suffer lies in the realm of the humanities. It was not caused by scientists and engineers and will never be destroyed by them.

Between a naturalistic philosophy reducing man wholly to the flux of nature and a humanistic philosophy emphasizing his distinctive humanity the conflict is real and, in the end, irreconcilable. But between science and the humanities there can be no real conflict whatever. That men in these two broad domains can come together in mutual respect was indicated, for instance, a number of years ago in a public statement. Fifteen distinguished American scientists (including such names as Walcott, Osborn, Conklin, Pupin, Mayo, Millikan) issued a joint statement with a similar group of religious leaders and men of affairs, regretting the antagonism between men in the domains of science and the humanities, specifically religion. They declared: *"The purpose of science is to develop, without prejudice or preconception of any kind, a knowledge of the facts, the laws, and the processes of nature. The even more important task of religion, on the other hand, is to develop the consciences, the ideals, and the aspirations of mankind."* The province of the one is natural knowledge; the province of the other is human values. So long as each stays within its bounds there can be no conflict. They are complementary, and should be co-operative. We need to know *what is,* we need to know *what ought to be,* and we need to know how they may be related.

To say that science is concerned with judgments of fact and not with judgments of value is not, however, to deny that implications of value enter into science. It is precisely because of the value implications of science that the humanistic spirit wholeheartedly supports science. The human values implied and presupposed by science are twofold.

First, it is animated by the passion to know, the quest of knowledge for its own sake. There is no science save as men produce it, and men produce it because they value it as men. Among the "aspirations of mankind" mentioned above, we must assign a high place to the desire for knowledge, including knowledge of nature—the physical and biological constitution and environment of our species. To this aspiration science owes its existence, as Dr. Einstein reminds us in a passage I have quoted. To this aspiration science also owes its capacity to survive. Whenever the aspiration for truth for its own sake declines, science also declines. This happened, for instance, when a Nazi leadership sought to evoke the miracle of a "German science." American men of science were revolted by this perversion not as scientists (science revolts at nothing) but as humanists. The humanistic spirit has, as one of its first and finest attributes, a passion for the disinterested, impartial pursuit of truth. In the process of education it is communicated with difficulty, and demands time and hard work. Yet innumerable college graduates can say of some scientist what one of them, for example, said of his beloved teacher of zoology, Henry V. Wilson, who "first revealed to my hazy young mind the fact that there was a vast field of knowledge where Truth, within certain recognizable limits, was not a matter of opinion, nor of taste, nor a recollection of historical facts, but a thing of demonstrable law. . . . He is the embodiment of the scientific spirit which seeks Truth always, without prejudices, without preconceptions, not caring where the search leads but careful always that in the utmost detail the distinction be preserved between that which is known and that which is supposed." Now, this distinction is one which is nowhere so impressively communicated as in the sciences of nature, which consequently merit an important place in liberal education.

Secondly, science is animated by the desire for use. Knowledge is not only an end in itself, but a means to further ends. As Francis Bacon taught, knowledge is power, and may be aimed at "the relief of man's estate," "inventions that may in some degree subdue and overcome the necessities and miseries of humanity" and also, we may add, contribute to man's chances of happiness. Science is thus instrumental in the achieving of values already defined by the humanistic spirit. For a hundred years the instrumental service of science has tended to obscure its intrinsic value, so that T. H. Huxley complained, as long ago as 1866, that science had been degraded to "a sort of comfort-grinding machine." On the intellectual plane the same tendency has led to a whole philosophy of instrumentalism, associated with the name of John Dewey. The motivation of this philosophy is human purpose, action, advantage, working experimentally in the overcoming of difficulties, and by a strange inversion truth itself is conceived as serviceability. This conclusion is not acceptable to the disinterested pursuit of truth which we call science. As W. T. Stace has said, "The ideal of the scientific mind has been, throughout the history of the west from Greek times to the present day, not to appraise theories by their capacity for helping human beings, but by their correspondence with the facts of the objective world. Of course science has sought, among other things, to discover truths which shall be of service to men. But it is a monstrous perversion to suggest that the quality of being serviceable to men is what, in the opinion of science, has rendered its discoveries true."

The humanistic spirit, believing in the pursuit of truth as an end in itself, believing also in the use of truth as a means to further ends, must hereafter give unstinted support to the great sciences of nature set in motion by the Hellenic mind and accelerated enormously by our own age. What is to be said of the so-called sciences of man?

The social sciences are relatively new and undeveloped subjects. With the exception of political science, heir of a political philosophy already mature as far back as Plato and Aristotle, the sciences of man in society came into being only a century or two ago—economics in the eighteenth century, anthropology, sociology, and social psychology in the late nineteenth century. As a distinct group or academic division comparable to the natural sciences and the humanities, they date from the present century. They owe their existence, in the form in which we have them, mainly to a belief that the objectives and methods of the triumphant natural sciences should next be applied to the study of human society. In the words of a committee report, "in social science, as in other sciences, an attempt is made to describe, rather than to evaluate, the subject matter. The goal is to understand the social order, to discover important concrete facts, and to find regularities that may be assumed to obtain beyond the cases observed and described." A social scientist, emulating the impartiality of the natural scientist, is not in a position to choose, for example, between democracy and fascism, either in his studies or in his teaching. He is permitted no preferences, no fixed standards, no absolute values. "As a scientist," says Robert M. Mac Iver, "he must be content with his world of relative values. Whatever his own convictions may be, he must be constantly alert not to impose them on the changeful order of things."

The impulse is admirable, but the results have been disappointing, and the suspicion is growing that methods and concepts drawn from natural science will not suffice for social science. The "wavering and incalculable behavior" of man, in the phrase of F. W. Taussig, suggests the enormous difficulty of a true science of man. The concept of cause and effect, as it appears in natural science, seems not to carry over to social science. Unlike other animate beings man is purposive, with a will that seems like the wind's will of the poet. Besides, while social behavior may be observed with a good deal of precision, the attempt to generalize the facts in the form of hypotheses cannot lead to positive results because the scientific method of controlled experiment and verification is not available. The result is a prevailing haziness and sense of frustration. "Twenty years hence," said Torrens in regard to political economy, "there will scarcely exist a doubt respecting any of its fundamental principles." Twenty years passed, one hundred and twenty years passed, and today the air is filled with more doubts than ever. Perhaps the best summary of the struggle of the social sciences to find themselves is that of Roscoe Pound, who begins by saying that he has no quarrel with them, having taught jurisprudence for forty years from the sociological standpoint. "But I do not deceive myself," he says, "as to those so-called sciences. So far as they are not descriptive, they are in continual flux. In the nature of things they cannot be sciences in the sense of physics or chemistry or astronomy. They have been organized as philosophies, have been worked out on the lines of geometry, have been remade to theories of history, have had their period of positivism, have turned to social psychology, and are now in an era of neo-Kantian methodology in some hands and of economic determinism or psychological realism or relativist skepticism or phenomenonological intuitionism in other hands. They do not impart wisdom; they need to be approached with acquired wisdom.... They are not foundation subjects. They belong in the superstructure."

How the social sciences are eventually to find themselves and to establish themselves as an essential part of liberal education, I shall not venture to suggest. One thing, however, seems very clear. They will have to derive their methodology from their own subject matter, rather than from the natural sciences. Since their subject matter is man, they may be expected to draw closer to the humanities. Even the "dismal science" of economics—dismal in its vicious circle of "producing wealth to produce more wealth"—is capable of taking on a profound human relevance in the hands of a man like John Ruskin, who does not look so foolish as he did in the good old days of classical political economy. A university professor wrote to me: "We economists too often stress some mechanical adjustment of prices or production when the real need is men of character and insight who can direct and enlighten us." Is there any reason why economists should not themselves be men of character and insight? In point of fact, the researches of our social scientists are largely directed by concepts of human values, despite professions of innocence. But the values are casually assumed, derived from the climate of opinion rather than earned by study and hard reflection. The social scientist of the future, one may venture to predict, will be obliged to bring his subject into more fruitful relation with the humanities, perhaps even to restore it to its humane matrix.

The curriculum of foundation studies, then, will be drawn mainly from the natural sciences and the humanities: the physical and the biological sciences, history, literature, art, and philosophy. It will offer, not hasty encyclopedic surveys of these fields, but a rich and intimate knowledge and experience of the best that man has learned and said and done in them. It will address the student, not as a future technician and specialist, but as a human being interested in understanding himself and his world. In this new task it cannot be expected to succeed until scholars in each subject have reconceived their aims and methods in the manner proposed, for one subject, by a recent collaborative book on *Literary Scholarship: Its Aims and Methods*. Only then will it be possible for us to undertake profitably the search for the concrete program of subjects and courses which will constitute the modern Great Curriculum equal in solidity and authority to the great curricula of past ages.

Reform within the subjects, if it has not advanced far, has at least begun. While it continues, we may welcome serious reflection upon the more general problem, as in the article by William C. DeVane on "American Education After the War," the book entitled *Liberal Education Re-Examined* by a committee appointed by the American Council of Learned Societies, and the book on *The Rebirth of Liberal Education* written by Fred B. Millett for the Rockefeller Foundation. We may welcome the ferment of curricular thought working everywhere today in our colleges and universities even though so much of it seems only frivolously modish and leads only to a meaningless tinkering dictated by political motives. Yet there is a danger that our preoccupation with curricula and organization and teaching procedures, in a word with machinery, will obscure the real problem. That problem, as I have tried to show, is the spirit and aim of the men who do the teaching, the faculty's philosophy of life and of education, which should give direction to all the practical decisions that must be made. A naturalistic philosophy has led the modern world, in totalitarian and democratic nations alike, toward a materialistic chaos and a resurgence of barbarism. An age of science has become an age of the misuse of science. Whether the forces of darkness will be halted no man can say. But this one can affirm: that if America is to play a high and civilizing role in the rest of the twentieth century, it will need a humanistic philosophy of life based on the concept of the dignity of man, and a humanistic philosophy of education that will supply our democratic society with men and women of intelligence and character.

9. The Great Faculty

Curricular legerdemain is no substitute for a change of heart and mind in the professoriate. What we are suffering from today is not so much a trivialized curriculum as a trivialized faculty. The only fundamental way to improve the curriculum is to improve the faculty which designs the curriculum. What William Penn said of government may be said, by paraphrase, of education: "Education rather depends upon Men, than Men upon Education. Let Men be good, and the Education can't be bad; if it be ill, they will cure it." No educational institution is any better than the men who do its work. This is why, in a report to the Carnegie Foundation on graduate school education, Marcia Edwards cancelled out most of her data by admitting that no plans or procedures can take the place of a competent staff in its eventual effect on education. This we have always known, or should have known. Even an egregiously bad procedure in graduate education, such as that in the field of English and comparative literature at Harvard before the First World War, achieved a large measure of success because the staff included such men as Kittredge, Babbitt, Neilson, Perry, Baker, Briggs, Rand, who transcended the procedure. In Harvard's undergraduate education the procedure was equally bad, the elective system being still in full swing, but again these great teachers, and others like them in other departments, saved the situation. Today, instead of proliferating procedures, plans, experiments, and disappointments, we would do well to begin by reforming the faculty.

The quality of the faculty depends, in the unwritten constitution of the state university, upon the administrators who appoint the professors. When a vacancy arises, what sort of professor do they look for? They look, sometimes hastily, more often persistently, for a specialist of high repute, i.e., high repute among other specialists. Incidentally, they inquire whether the specialist scholar is also a good teacher or at least not a bad one. Incidentally, they consider his personality, being satisfied if it is superficially agreeable. They display no concern for his character so long as he has done nothing scandalous, and they have no interest whatever in the values he lives by. A good professor is simply a good specialist in his particular field.

The results are deplorable. Administrators are not pleased with their own handiwork, students can admire only a few of their teachers, and even the faculty of specialists is aware that specialism is not enough. In its 1933 report on the state of teaching, the American Association of University Professors acknowledged that their own profession is failing to attract to itself "a sufficient number of broadly cultured young men and women," because faculty members are not "portraying by their own careers and example to the younger generation of scholars the kind of profession which strikes the youthful imagination in a favorable light when compared with other callings." The examples are so bad that they are not worthy of imitation.

The examples offered by the state university faculty are mainly of three types: pedants, dilettanti, and career-builders. It goes without saying that the types are not always distinct from each other, nor without some of the admirable traits of a fourth type, the relatively few examples of "Man Thinking." The first type, the pedants, have often been publicly exposed. They have knowledge without the power of it. Their interest in facts and technique is fussy, their results are mostly trifling. In their dull and honest incapacity, they do not well know the difference between the important and the unimportant. They often base their claims for promotion on the number of pages they have published. They impress some administrators, but generally they are regarded as dead wood, of which, it must be confessed, a large part of the academic forest is made up.

Smaller in numbers but more conspicuous are the dilettanti. Some of them are dabblers pure and simple, but as a rule they maintain respectability by publishing as pedants or scholars while teaching as dilettanti: charmers, entertainers, showmen, even clowns. Too often they are swindlers, offering education, in their easygoing way, at cut prices and thus cheating both their students and their employers; or else sentimentalists, pitying the dull and harried student and grading him well above his deserts. By such meretricious practices the dilettanti manage to be "popular," which, according to Emerson, "is to go down perpendicularly." In academic rank and salary they are more likely to go up.

Most successful of all are the career-builders. These are the specialists who "play the game." They are not the dedicated spirits, the absent-minded and unworldly professors, of popular myth. They have no vocation in the fine old sense of a call or summons to a particular occupation. They show with painful clearness that faculty members can be all too "human," that is to say, "natural." Emerson knew them: "Men, such as they are, very naturally seek money or power." The career-builders may be subdivided into two further types. One type comprises the go-getters, the Machiavellians, who subordinate principle to politics. Aggressive party men with a cynical view of human nature, they support the administration of set purpose and shoulder their way ahead of scrupulous colleagues by evasion, treachery, defamation, and the like. They are gifted in cooperation with each other but are quite ready, when need arises, to cut the throat of a fellow go-getter who gets in the way. The other type comprises the more passive yes-men, who, suppressing inner dissent, seek to advance themselves by appeasement: by hypocritical flattery, or a timid and time-serving acquiescence, or an unnatural silence. Emerson recognized them when he charged that "the scholar is decent, indolent, complaisant." Protected by security of tenure, this type of professor is nevertheless too timorous to avail himself of his academic freedom, though only academic freedom can justify security of tenure. In general it is the career-builders, the mass of go-getters and yes-men, who determine what goes on in the university and who are most richly rewarded by the administration.

The admirable exceptions are far too few: young men whose inner resources are such that they will risk much rather than merely play the game, and older men who have learned that life without principle is not really life. In every university faculty there is a minority of dedicated scholars and teachers, who have not permitted their specialties to rob them of their manhood, who are persons as well as instruments, who are devoted to whatsoever things are true and elevated and just, who are laboring in behalf of liberal education and humane scholarship in the hostile environment of a materialistic institution. They are examples of Man Thinking, man devoted to ideas. They are lovers of knowledge ("science," in the old general sense) and lovers of wisdom ("philosophers"). They are "academic" in the sense that they would have been able to hold their own in Plato's Academy. They have the independent mind, the critical spirit, being above their knowledge not beneath it. They are thus, on a higher plane, like the liberally educated student. Combining broad understanding and concentrated knowledge, they relate their special subjects to tangent subjects, to all subjects. They relate past and present, and make both live. They deal thoughtfully with the whole of life, and with life as a whole, having committed themselves to a philosophy—and perhaps a religion as well—worthy of the dignity of man, though there is great diversity among them in doctrine. They are men of character as well as intelligence—men of integrity, not conflicting pieces of men, acting in all things (within the limits of human frailty) with sincerity, fairness, friendliness, and courage. Free and brave, they can say with Emerson, "We will walk on our own feet; we will work with our own hands; we will speak our own minds."

Such are the exceptional scholar-teachers, at their rare best. With them we must be content to subsume admirable types wanting this completeness. Some are admirable because of their personal character, the fine quality of their actual living, though their minds may not be speculative. Others are admirable for the depth and richness of their inner life, or spiritual insight. Others, again, are exceptional for their highly vitalized intellectual life, their energy in forming and relating ideas, or in using erudition for high ends, or in applying standards of value. All of these types, without trying to be exemplary, are aware that values are "caught" more than taught, that the best teaching is always teaching by example, that what motivates students, and motivates them in the right direction, is excellence of mind and character in the teacher. This is not too much to ask of a university professor. He need not be a "great man" or a "genius." He need be great only in what he represents—the humanistic spirit in action.

Every faculty, as I have said, contains a minority of such men. In the eyes of a naturalistic administration, they constitute a sort of opposition party. Sometimes they are viewed intolerantly as a barrier to be forced down, sometimes tolerantly as a means of stimulating intellectual virility in the faculty as a whole. Their numbers are few. But the reform of the faculty will not be in sight till they are many.

The head of a department can do something to increase their numbers. A humanistic head, in one department or another, can assist the dean in the appointment and promotion of the right sort of men, because the dean, as likely as not, will not know the difference between the right sort and the wrong sort. Many a dean, concentrating upon a man's competence as a specialist—his reputation in "his own field"—will accept recommendations of men who, it will turn out, will enlarge the minority. A humanistic head, while giving due weight to specialized competence, will not let himself be misled by "fields." For example, he will prefer an enlightened specialist in Renaissance history to a narrow specialist in American history, even when the so-called vacancy is in the latter field, for what he seeks above all is to gather a group of humane scholars. He will remember that, beneath a scholar's knowledge, guiding the use of that knowledge in teaching and productive scholarship, is his outlook on life, his scale of values. Like William James (at the opening of the first lecture on *Pragmatism*) he will number himself with those who believe, with Chesterton, that "The most practical and important thing about a man is still his view of the universe. We think that for a landlady considering a lodger it is important to know his income, but still more important to know his philosophy. We think that for a general about to fight an enemy it is important to know the enemy's numbers, but still more important to know the enemy's philosophy." In the same way an intelligent department head, considering a scholar and teacher of youth, will find it important to know the man's achievement in learning but still more important to know his underlying philosophy—not so much his formal opinions but rather the values he actually lives by as man and scholar.

In recommending new appointments the department head will desire the fullest evidence of ability, taking into account repeated interviews, the testimony of judges carefully selected for their humanistic standards (not for their names or high place), the quality of publications when closely analyzed, the test of an actual lecture or series of lectures or a temporary summer appointment. He will spare no effort, because he knows that a department, like a university, is not courses or procedures or books or laboratories but men. Once he has found and brought the right men, he will spare no effort to keep them. He will try to assure a wide opening for their talents by dropping the untalented—

> Enow of such as, for their bellies' sake,
> Creep, and intrude, and climb into the fold!

As he comes to know his best men intimately, to understand their natural interests and capacities, he will assign them to tasks which will call forth their creative endeavor. He will give them the courses, committee duties, administrative functions, most likely to develop their abilities, and then let them alone in the spirit of the Middle English proverb: "Send the wise and say no thing." If they have a special gift for productive scholarship, he will do everything possible to protect their time and energies. Since the tasks of a department are numerous, he will welcome diversity in excellence, never seeking to mold the staff to his own image. Free of envy, he will be glad if some of his professors are better than he. In a few state universities where heads have more responsibility than deans, the head will encourage the right men by promotions in salary and rank. In the great majority of institutions, he will do all he can to see that merit, as he understands it, is recognized and rewarded by the administration.

10. The Great Administration

An occasional department head, guided by some such ideal, can do something to increase the humanistic minority. But the general complexion of the faculty is determined, of course, by the administration, by the deans and president who select the department heads and hold the purse strings involved in all appointments and promotions. In a naturalistic university the deans and president are nearly always themselves naturalistic in outlook. To a large extent the university is naturalistic because its leadership is. If it is to become humanistic its leadership will have to be humanistic. We must consequently go on to ask, What sort of leadership is worthy of the place of power in a university?

The qualifications would appear to be closely similar to those of the faculty. The administrator in a humanistic university is, like a sound leader in a political democracy, one of Jefferson's "men of intelligence and character." He will have the type of intelligence appropriate to a university: himself liberally educated, he will have taught with success in a college or university faculty, and will have had, preferably, experience in a lesser administrative position (there is an old saying, quoted by Bacon, that "A place showeth the man"). He will have the traits of character ascribed, above, to the professor, together with consideration and patience in dealing with a faculty which contains his equals and perhaps superiors. He will wish to lead and not drive. He will never use democratic processes as a cloak for the use of force. Courage he will need more than the professor, since his tenure is insecure. Justice may prove costly to him, but in the end injustice would be costlier. He will be mindful of the warning that power corrupts, the more because his position carries great power.

So great is the power lodged in his hands, according to the American system, that a university president can easily become a dictator. If he assumes all the responsibilities implied by his office, he is likely to turn out either a benevolent autocrat or the builder of a sinister power machine. If he prefers to neglect his responsibilities and to become a decorative nonentity ("stuffed shirt," as the elegant phrase goes), his subordinates will be dictators. If he believes in democracy and uses democratic processes as much as the system permits, because he knows that the Great Faculty is a free faculty, he will find the logic of the system against him. The basic fact in the university constitution is that he, the president, ultimately controls the entire budget. How much independence would the United States Senate have if every senator's salary were fixed by the will of a Vice-President appointed by the President? If it is easy for a university head (or his delegates) to play the role of dictator, it is exceedingly hard if not impossible for him to play the role of democratic leader.

Such a system is not in harmony with American democracy, nor is it necessary. University government was highly democratic in Europe, before the New Order, even in countries whose polities were largely autocratic. Sooner or later we shall have to reconsider our system. But till then, under the existing system, the president of a university will continue to have the responsibility of guiding its development through the officers and teaching staff that he appoints. This responsibility he cannot avoid. If, in derogation of his duty, he delegates professorial appointments entirely to his deans, he must still appoint the deans, or, which is the same thing, accept those he has inherited. Whether he attempts much or little or nothing, he cannot avoid exercising an influence so strong that it determines the character of the institution. The character of the institution, we have said, depends on men. He selects the men. As they are, so will the university be. Thus through the president, the university is, as William Ernest Hocking has said, "authoritative in a peculiarly indirect, difficult, and dangerous manner; namely, in the choice of the teaching staff." There is something less than candor, for instance, in the motto heading a department of the *Record* published by Teachers College, Columbia: "Teachers College, as an institution, holds no position, advocates no theory of education. It selects its faculty and, as every such institution must, permits each member untrammeled to present whatever his reflections and his researches lead him to believe." The disarming piety of tone in this statement does not conceal the vital phrase which destroys the piety: *"It selects its faculty."*

Even Thomas Jefferson, father of the State University of Virginia, was obliged to recognize the indoctrination implied by the selection of a faculty, and was willing to accept the responsibility for sound indoctrination, according to his lights. Writing to Madison, he said very frankly: "In the selection of our Law Professor, we must be rigorously attentive to his political principles." Blackstone, as Jefferson conceived, caused the legal profession "to slide into toryism, and nearly all the young brood of lawyers now are of that hue. They suppose themselves, indeed, to be whigs, because they no longer know what whigism or republicanism means. It is in our seminary that that vestal flame is to be kept alive; it is thence to spread anew over our own and the sister States. If we are true and vigilant in our trust, within a dozen or twenty years a majority of our own legislature will be from one school, and many disciples will have carried its doctrines home with them to their several States, and will have leavened thus the whole mass." Was this a fascist zeal for *Gleichschaltung?* Or was it a desire to accept responsibility to "make reason and the will of God prevail" through the orderly process of appointment? Should Jefferson have chosen a law professor of the hue of toryism—especially if the best tory was abler than the best whig? If a number of law professors were to be chosen, should they have been tories or whigs, or dominantly one or the other? or should the selection have been neutral, without regard for hue? In the last case the selection might have been neutral but the result would not have been: since nearly all the young brood of lawyers were tories who supposed themselves to be whigs, Jefferson would have had a tory law school.

Jefferson's problem was difficult, more difficult than that which confronts the president of a state university today in the situation I have indicated. It is not imperative for him to know whether a professor he is considering is a Republican or a Democrat, an Episcopalian or a Methodist. A state university is not committed to any particular party or denomination. What I have termed the general intent of the university is not a particular intent. The general intent involves, broadly, a philosophy of life, and the choice lies between a naturalistic and a humanistic philosophy. Toward which of the two is the president to guide the university through his appointment and promotion of officers and teaching staff? Like Jefferson, he cannot be neutral, since the great majority of the old brood and the young brood in the American academic world are naturalists, even when they suppose themselves to be humanists. To try to be neutral means to side with the naturalists. If the president closes his eyes to all qualifications except ability and reputation (and that is what he commonly does) he will continue to have a naturalistic university.

Let us suppose that the president wishes to change the complexion and intent of his university, to encourage the growth in it of a humanistic spirit. Has he any chance of success? As President Conant has rightly said, "Over a period of years the new appointments and promotions to permanent positions determine the fate of any college or university." If the direction of change is to be humanistic, this statement applies above all to the arsenal of the humanistic spirit, the university's college of liberal arts. First must come the appointment of a suitable dean of the college. Then, in a period of say ten years, there will be an opportunity to refill many headships and other key positions, to promote many men to full professorships, to promote many assistant professors to permanent positions, to reconstitute the large group of assistant professors, and to try out perhaps hundreds of instructors and assistants. Above all, the president and the dean will study closely the younger men, who are in the main the university of the future. At the end of ten years, if the administration has made the faculty its main business and has reached its innumerable decisions wisely, the result will be a university dominantly humanistic.

This is not a proposal of uniformity, which has no place in a state or any other university. Men who have the humanistic spirit are anything but alike; they enjoy disagreeing with each other as much as disagreeing with the naturalists. Nor will the faculty be made up of them alone. "Dominantly humanistic" is not exclusively humanistic. If uniformity became a danger, the administration should of set purpose introduce professors who would assure a healthy difference of outlook. But the danger is unreal. The old guard of naturalists would remain, by virtue of permanent tenure, and would be tolerated because the humanistic spirit is itself tolerant. Besides, it is far from easy today to find men who are of the kind desired, and even if it were not, many mistakes would be made, and many men would turn out to be other than was supposed, or would gradually alter their outlook. All of this the administration would accept with the best grace because the humanistic spirit is not only tolerant but humble, never too sure of its rightness.

A grave difficulty remains. Granted that a good president could bring about a reorientation in this way, how is a state university, unless it already has such a leader, to acquire one?

The choice of a president, under the American system of university government, is made by a governing board of trustees or regents. This is the most important action for which the board is responsible. In theory, to be sure, according to *A Manual for Trustees* by Raymond M. Hughes, "the control of policy is a function of the trustees," who "'should determine what sort of an institution they control." But in actual practice the functions of the board appear to be twofold: directly guiding the life of the university in its business aspects, and indirectly guiding the life of the university in its intellectual and spiritual aspects by the selection of a president. In carrying out the former function the board is usually astute, because it is made up largely of business men; in carrying out the latter function it is usually inept, for the same reason.

The trustees of a state university, it is true, are recruited from the best citizens of the state. They are successful men and women—intelligent, alert, earnest in behalf of the public good, hearty in their belief in democracy and in education. But their experience of life, while it has qualified them for understanding the complexities of business and legal affairs, has not qualified them for understanding the very different complexities of higher education. When, usually but once during their tenure, they are confronted by their responsibility of naming a president, they find themselves sadly unprepared. Their criteria in making a selection are as inadequate as those of a university faculty would be if called upon to name the president of a great industrial corporation. They often look for the "business man" type, which they understand, or an effective "money raiser" (but will he spend the money wisely?), or a man with a good "front" and ability in public speaking, or an "expert in education"—i.e. a man with the Teachers College mind. The net result is that they are likely to choose more men from "Education" than any other field, and more men from outside than inside the liberal arts faculty. The one type which they almost never look for and hence almost never come upon is the type I have described, the man of intelligence and character who understands liberal education and is imbued with the humanistic spirit.

However ill qualified for their task, governing boards could do better than they have done. Busy though they necessarily are with their private affairs, some of the members of a board might give more serious thought to the problems of education. If the humanistic tradition interested them, they could seek to understand the essential principles of humane education by reading, toward this end, *The Republic* of Plato, *Aristotle on Education* (edited by John Burnet), Elyot's *Book of the Governor*, Newman's *Idea of a University*, Arnold's *Culture and Anarchy*, and then some recent American books such as those by Flexner, Hutchins, Van Doren, Greene *et al.*, Millett, and the essays by seven writers which I have brought together in a little volume entitled *The Humanities After the War*. It is perhaps a fair guess that few state university trustees are really familiar with half the books in any such list. Then, for advice, they should go to the best judges they can find, e.g., alumni whose standards can be respected, administrators and professors in small colleges who appear to be genuinely liberal in outlook, and men of breadth and understanding in various occupations, such as scientists, churchmen, authors, editors. If only two or three members of a governing board made an earnest effort to comprehend what is at stake, to determine the right criteria, and to seek advice in the right places, they would be able to exert a strong influence upon their less active colleagues. They might succeed in getting the board to name a president who was, at least, not hostile to the humanistic spirit.

But in fact most governing boards will continue to name presidents as they have been doing. Naturalistic and utilitarian boards will give us naturalistic and utilitarian presidents. Only occasionally and by chance will they select a man competent to lead the way toward a university whose general intent is humanistic. What foresight failed to do a happy accident may do. Here and there we may expect a president to be chosen who will see his opportunity to demonstrate what such a university is and what it can accomplish for society. He will attract plenty of attention. Puzzled and rudderless as they are, our institutions of higher education turn with the keenest interest to any demonstration or experiment, such as the Meiklejohn experiment, the General College at Minnesota, the Chicago College Plan, St. John's College, in which somebody (*mirabile dictu*) seems to have a clearly defined purpose. One or two demonstrations of a humanistic state university would be a wonder among wonders in the eyes of those who are without standards and are looking for possible "trends" to adjust themselves to. It might even start a new trend.

In the long run public opinion will determine whether we shall have the humanistic university. If there is to be a great curriculum, a great faculty, a great administration, there must be a Great Society. Broad movements of thought and desire, rising to clearness in our society as time goes on, will decide whether the naturalistic philosophy of life and education is the wave of the future, or whether a humanistic philosophy will give a new direction to life and education. The formation of public opinion, in a democracy, is an exceedingly complicated matter. But one thing is plain: universities need not wait passively for its formation. They are themselves formers of public opinion. They not only reflect trends, they also start and accelerate them. University faculties contain a majority of the intellectuals of this country, and certainly the intellectuals are agents in shaping the public mind and will. They originate doctrines and attitudes, pass them on to their students, and, through the students as well as directly, reach the general public. University thinkers, writers, and scientists have had an incalculable influence in the making of the world we live in today, and can have the same influence in the making of the world of tomorrow. Are they prepared for this high responsibility? More and more of them are being stirred to creative thought by the crisis of our times, but the great majority have not yet emerged from the apathy of the period between the wars.

Are the designated leaders of the faculties, are the presidents of the state universities, prepared any better? Unhappily they seem to be lagging behind both the faculties and the public. With few exceptions they stand helpless and bewildered, devoid of critical and creative thought, unable to imagine a revitalized university, repeating the clichés of yesterday's education. This is the impression given, at all events, by the report on Postwar Educational Problems, issued in 1944, by a committee of the National Association of State Universities. The report frankly admits that the state universities, in the depression crisis of the 1930's, "failed to do what they should have done": failed "to consider the fundamental questions." For this discreditable reason, "the problems that confront us today are essentially the same problems that confronted us a decade ago.... Are we going to miss our second opportunity to face these problems squarely?" Apparently we are, judging from the report, which can only be called a model of futility. It is devoid of intellectual virility. It proposes the old conflicting objectives and the old impossible means of attaining them. It abounds in the old claptrap about motivation, individual differences, student advising, teaching methods, measurement of achievement, and the like. It is written in a manner self-conscious, pretentious, complacent, and condescending. And it contains fantastic passages, phrased as if for low IQ's, such passages as those on the dictionary definition of "to plan," on glaciers and mastodons, on hospital patients and their trays, which one might enjoy as satire of administrative inanity were they not offered in all seriousness. At the close the report reminds us, quite rightly, that state universities depend for their support upon public taxation and hence upon public opinion. "We must therefore subject education to critical analysis before less skillful persons invade our province." But the way to invasion is left wide open. One can only hope that the persons invading will be not less but more skillful.

One can hope this with some confidence, for public opinion is today sounder than administrative opinion. It is more likely to ask the fundamental questions and face them squarely. It has a stronger feeling for the essentials of education, for a "common core" of knowledge and abilities as a means of self-realization and social unity. Less swayed by the relativities that obsess the academic mind, the public is inclined to the belief that essentials are always essentials, good at all times. Despite its seeming inertness it looks for leadership, in education as in politics, which can inspire it with purposes a little above its ordinary self. It contains many thoughtful citizens who will demand better state universities as soon as the period of emergency is over. What sort of period will follow, no man can say. At the worst it will repeat the disillusionment that came after the First World War, but it will hardly repeat the blindness and apathy. The second and greater war has shown that America is in the world, in a very dangerous world. If the American public is realistic enough to accept universal military training if it seems necessary as a measure of safety, it may well be realistic enough to accept a solider education for the same purpose. For it seems clear that, whether the new era is to be one of international co-operation or international anarchy, we shall need a stronger democracy than we have had, better disciplined in body and mind. Such a program will necessitate a more liberal education, in which the humanities will be regarded as "builders of morale," once these subjects have got themselves ready for such a role.

To underestimate the public is a more serious blunder than to overestimate it. Let those who are planning the state universities of tomorrow remember this. An educational leadership of cynicism and fear will solve nothing. An educational leadership of faith and courage may be defeated in the end, but it is better to be defeated in the end than at the beginning.

www.ingramcontent.com/pod-product-compliance
Lightning Source LLC
Chambersburg PA
CBHW031715230426
43668CB00006B/216